Learn Magic
with Jim Stott

About The Author

Jim Stott has been successfully entertaining children and adults with his magic since 1976. With 40+ years of experience, he knows and understands his audiences. With six kids and thirteen grandkids, Jim knows children. Add to that his experience as a teacher, principal, and school superintendent and you know that you will be in good hands learning magic from Jim.

Jim not only performs magic but teaches other magicians how to entertain as well. He is the author of Birthday Magicology, which is a twelve week course teaching magicians how to achieve success in performing birthday parties and Restaurant Magicology, which teaches magicians how to perform successfully in restaurant settings.

Jim is a member of the *Society of American Magicians*, *Kidabra International*, and the *International Brotherhood of Magicians*. He is a two-time president of the *Society of American Magicians* (Jay Marshall Assembly #148 in Chicago) and has been recognized as a Life Member of the *Society of American Magicians*.

To learn more about Jim, visit his website at
www.JimStottMagic.com

Links:
www.BirthdayMagicology.com
www.RestaurantMagicology.com

Jim Stott
AGIC

Rules for Good Magicians

Helpful Hints... Practicing

Make practice easier by setting aside a certain time each day, maybe just after dinner, for practicing your tricks and routines.

Keep going for about 15 minutes, then stop for about 5 or 10 minutes. This would be a good time to think about the kind of story you'll tell when you do the trick.

Now practice the same trick again for another 15 minutes. You'll find the moves are easier to do after that short break.

It's a good idea to practice the trick and the story you'll tell at the same time.

When you perform a routine in front of people, you may be nervous. This is normal. However, when you have practiced the routine as much as possible, you won't be quite as nervous, because you'll have a better idea of what's going to happen.

Magician Ethics

If you see a magician do a good trick, don't ask them how they did it. Just because you're a magician doesn't mean they have to tell you.

If you are watching a magic show, and you think you know the secret to a trick, DON'T say you know how it was done. You may think this makes you look smart, but it is actually very rude. People are at the show to have a good time, not to find out what tricks you know. Be a polite audience!

SECRETS: Never, never tell your friends how you did a trick; no matter how much they ask. Once they learn the secrets, all the fun is gone. When they ask, be polite and say "I promised never to tell", or "I don't know how it works myself!"

REPEATING: Never do the same trick again right away. When your friends say "Do that again", it means they were fooled, but this time they'll catch you. If you do it again, their eyes will be watching every move. If they insist, do a different trick.

REACTION: Your audience will be surprised when the magic happens. So when the magic trick happens, Instead of boasting about how good you are, act surprised as well.

PRACTICE: Practice each trick many times before you show it to anyone. If you show it without practicing, you'll just give the secret away or have the trick fail. If you do mess up a trick in front of an audience, just do another trick.

MIRRORS: Always think about how the trick will look to the audience. The best way is to practice in front of a mirror or video camera, so you can see what your friends will see. They will watch closely, so you must know how it looks to them. Sometimes you will see things that surprise you and need to be fixed.

TRICKS: Choose the tricks you like best. Nobody could do every trick equally well. As you try new tricks, some will "feel" right for you, while others won't. Stick to the ones that feel right, and you will do them the best. Always add your personality.

www.JimStottMagic.com

"FORCING" A CARD

THE SPECTATOR PICKS THE CARD YOU WANT, BUT THEY THINK IT'S THE CARD THEY WANT.

THE CUT FORCE

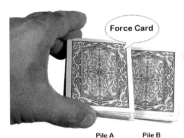

Before starting the trick, secretly remember the top card of the deck. This is the "force card" you will force your friend to choose.

Have the spectator lift up half the deck, and place it on the table.

You now have two piles of cards, A & B. The card your friend will choose, the force card, is on the top of pile A. Keep track of where the force card is.

Tell your friend you will mark where the cut was. Pick up pile B, and place it sideways on top of pile A like the image below.

Look at your friend, then tell her to show her card to everybody. You lift pile B and point to the top card of pile A. She will think this is where she cut the deck of cards, so when the card is picked up, everybody will think it is the one she chose.

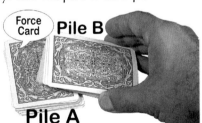

THE SCARF FORCE

Once again, secretly remember the top card of the deck. You will also need a scarf that you cannot see through. Hold the deck in your hand, and drape the scarf over it.

Here comes the important move. Under cover of the scarf, turn the deck upside-down in your hand. The photos are shown without the scarf. The spectator can not see it, since the hanky is covering it up, so he will think it is normal.

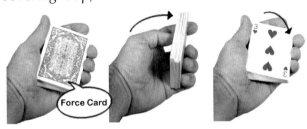

Now have the spectator lift up the top half of the deck.

Before the scarf uncovers your hand, turn the bottom half of the deck right-side up.

When the spectator takes the top card off the deck in your hand, he will think it is the chosen card.

Spectator

You

www.JimStottMagic.com

THE CASE OF THE CARD IN THE CASE

You'll need a deck of cards, one duplicate card, a way to vanish the card, and the card case (the box that the cards come in when purchased).

Here's what happens: The spectator picks a card, remembers it, and shows it to everyone. (It's ok if you see it). The card disappears, and reappears inside the card case, which was in full view at all times. This is a very strong routine, which people will remember for a long time.

How does it work? Have the duplicate card on top of the deck, inside the case. When you pull the deck out of the box, leave the duplicate inside. Keep the opening of the case towards you, so nobody sees you leave the card inside.

Lay the card case on the table, so everybody can see it (but keep the duplicate inside and hidden). Have the spectator choose a card, but make sure s/he gets the card which matches the one in the case. You'll need to force the card.

Here is where you vanish the card, but don't say you're going to vanish it. Just say you'll wrap it up for safe keeping.

Now say the magic words, wave the wand, jump up and down, or whatever. Show that the card is gone, then point to the card case. Tell one of the spectators to open it, and show the card inside.

www.JimStottMagic.com

THE PAPER BAG CARD TRICK

For this routine you'll need a paper bag that easily fits over a person's head, a deck of cards, a duplicate card, and some tape.

Have somebody choose a card from the deck, and show it around. Then you toss the deck (and card) into the paper bag, and shake them up. Reach into the bag and pull out a card... but it's the wrong one. Try again, but it's still wrong. Ask the spectator if he can find the card. Turn the paper bag upside down over the spectator's head. With the cards falling everywhere, ask if they've found it yet. Take the paper bag off their head, say "How could you miss it? It's the only card still in there", reach inside, and pull out the chosen card.

Here's how it's done. Inside the paper bag is a duplicate card, stuck to the bottom with a small piece of tape. When the spectator chooses a card, you force the card that matches the one in the paper bag. From here on it's acting. When you pull out the wrong cards, act really disappointed.

Make sure the person who wears the paper bag is in a good mood. When the routine is over, be certain to pick up the cards. Putting them back in the paper bag will make that easy.

Here is another idea. While looking in the bag for the chosen card, ask if it was red or black. Let's say it is red. When they answer red, pull out a card that is completely covered in red, with no numbers or anything showing. This should get a good laugh.

Here's how. Get the jokers, and with paint or marker, color them completely, then tape them in the bag next to the duplicate card.

Jim Stott
MAGIC
www.JimStottMagic.com

HELPFUL HINTS... CAN YOU SEE THIS?

Audiences need to see what you are doing. If you are doing tricks for a few people, they can be small tricks you can fit in your pocket. When you do a show for a large crowd, make sure the tricks can be seen by everybody. Card tricks are difficult for a large group, because people sitting in the back will not be able to see well.

Adjust your voice to suit the crowd also. For a few people, you can just talk normal. For a large group, you will need to talk louder. Don't yell, however, just talk louder.

Always keep in mind what the audience will be seeing. When you show them something, hold it at your finger tips, so everyone can see it clearly. Watch people in TV commercials when they hold something. They make sure it's easy to see. This is one of the reasons why practicing in front of a mirror is so important.

THE SHORT CARD KEY CARD

Many card tricks start with somebody choosing a card, looking at it, then putting it back. You must find the card. By using a short card, it is easy to find a chosen card. It takes a lot of PRACTICE, because you need to feel the card with your fingertips.

Trim about ¹/₁₆ inch off the top

A card is trimmed 1/16th of an inch shorter than all the others. This may not seem like much, but it makes a big difference when you riffle the ends of the deck. You may need an adults help with the trimming.

Next, using fingernail clippers, trim the corners so they match the other cards as closely as possible.

Trim top corners (with nail clippers) so they match the other corners

How do you riffle the cards? First, make sure the edges of the deck are perfectly flat. Tap it gently on a table to set them. Bend back one end of the deck, but not too far, or you will not be able to riffle correctly.

Softly let go of one card at a time. When you come to the short card, it will feel different, and if you are riffling correctly, it will automatically stop. You may also hear the "snap" when you hit the short card.

To use the short card to find a chosen card: Make sure the short card is on the bottom of the deck. Have a helper choose any card. Have her put the chosen card on top of the deck. Now tell her to cut the deck, and place the bottom half on top of the other half. That automatically places the short card on top of the chosen card. Try it and see!

Finding it is easy now. Just riffle the cards until you come to the short card. The chosen card will be the next one down. Easy!

A way to make this trick even better is to let your helper cut the deck as often as they want after they have inserted the chosen card. The short card should stay on top of the chosen card. If your helper cuts the deck between the short card and the chosen card, then the chosen card will be on top of the deck, and the short card will be on the bottom. If that happens, just cut the deck one more time, and the chosen and short card will be together again.

Sometimes you may have trouble finding the short card. This usually happens when the short card is near the top or bottom of the deck. Just cut the deck, and riffle again.

PRESTO!

WWW.JIMSTOTTMAGIC.COM

THE UPSIDE-DOWN CARD LOCATION

Ask a helper to choose any card from the deck. Show it around, then put it back in the deck. You try to find it, but can't. You spread the cards out, but one card is upside-down... it's the chosen card!

Here is how it works: Your helper picks any card she wants. If you want, the front of the card may be signed with a magic marker, so they can't forget the card. You then tell her to show the card to everyone, and to make sure you don't see it, you turn your back to the audience. Keep the deck of cards in your hands. Now comes the secret move.

Keep your elbows against your sides, so the audience can't see your arms move. Turn the deck upside-down, then turn the top card upside down. You now have a deck that looks normal even though it's actually upside-down.

When you turn around, hold the deck in your hand like before, and insert the chosen card into the deck. You've actually put the card into an upside-down deck, but the audience will think it's normal.

Announce you will find the card without looking, and hold the deck behind your back. Grab the top card (the one that's upside-down), show it to everyone, and ask if it was the chosen card. When they say no, look a little worried and say you'll try again.

Reach behind you and grab the next card, show it to everyone, and again they will say no. Now act like you really messed up the trick, and start spreading the cards apart like in the photo at the top of this page.

When you come to the upside down card, push it out onto the table, but keep your finger on it. Tell everybody that the card turned upside-down by magic.

Now ask your helper what the name of the card was, and when she says it, turn the card over and show it. Take a bow!

WWW.JIMSTOTTMAGIC.COM

CARD SPELLING

Before starting this trick, take the cards out of the deck that you see in the picture, and arrange them in order like the picture. Put the rest of the deck away.

It doesn't matter which suits are used (hearts, clubs, spades, diamonds). Don't let anybody watch you arrange the cards.

When you're done, turn the stack of cards (the packet) over in your hand and hold it just like normal.

Start with the top card (the 3), and spell the first card in the list (ACE), taking one card off the top for each letter, and putting that card on the bottom. Turn the next card over, and it will be the ace.

Place the ace on the table, face up so everybody can see it.

www.JimStottMagic.com

Now spell out the next card in the list, the TWO, putting each card on the bottom like before. Turn over the top card, and place it on the table. It will be the two. Continue with the rest of the packet. The list of cards to spell are:

- **ACE**
- **TWO**
- **THREE**
- **FOUR**
- **FIVE**
- **SIX**
- **SEVEN**
- **EIGHT**
- **NINE**
- **TEN**
- **JACK**
- **QUEEN**
- **KING**

To make this more entertaining, pretend you're not sure if it will work. Of course, you know by now it will work IF YOU PRACTICE!!

FOLDING PAPER GIMMICK

A torn card is folded into a piece of yellow paper. A newspaper is wrapped around that, and everybody says the magic words. When everything is unfolded, the card has magically been restored!

THE SECRET:

The yellow paper is actually 2 pieces glued back to back, each folded the same way.

Folded into the back side is a whole card, which matches the torn card. You'll need to use 2 decks. Make sure you have permission before tearing cards.

When unfolding the papers, be careful not to show the back of the yellow paper. Nobody should know it's double sided. Keep it sitting on the newspaper.

Have a helper tear the card. Now place the torn pieces in the center of the yellow paper. Carefully fold the yellow paper, while keeping it in the center of the newspaper.

Now comes the secret move. While folding the newspaper, simply turn over the yellow paper. The large size of the newspaper will help to cover this move. Practice this often so it will be done smoothly.

Unfold the papers and show the torn card is whole again!

These folded papers are a very useful tool for switching one flat item for another.

You could turn blank paper into a dollar bill, or 5 one dollar bills into 1 five dollar bill. You could use it to vanish a card, or make one appear.

A great bonus... it folds up small and can be carried in your pocket.

WWW.JIMSTOTTMAGIC.COM

The art of hand shadows, a form of puppetry, goes back many many years. Perhaps even to the time of cavemen sitting around a fire.

Today, however, you can use an electric light shining on a wall. By adjusting your hands in the shapes of the pictures, and holding them in front of the light, you can make shadows that seem to come alive.

This can be a fun way to tell stories, perhaps as part of a magic show routine itself.

These figures will take a lot of practice, although you won't need a mirror for obvious reasons. A video recorder may come in handy.

CANDY ON A ROPE

For this trick you will need a roll of Lifesavers™ (or any candy with a hole in the center), a handkerchief, and a length of string or thin rope.

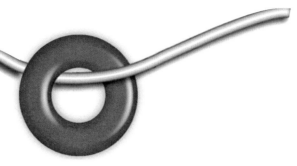

Here is how the trick looks. The piece of candy is on the string, like the picture shows. A handkerchief is draped over the string, hiding the candy. Both ends of the string are held by other people. The magician reaches under the handkerchief, and takes the candy off the string, seemingly without breaking the candy or the string!

How? Before you start the trick, when nobody is around, carefully break a piece of the candy. You may have to try a few to get a clean break.

Glue the two pieces back together with just a little bit of glue, and give it time to dry.

Make sure that this prepared candy is the first one in the roll, so it is the one you put on the string. When you reach under the handkerchief, have an extra piece of candy hidden in your hand. The best way to hide it is not to look at it. People tend to look where you look. Quietly break the candy on the string, and let it fall into your sleeve, or hold it hidden in your hand.

Now bring out the unbroken piece, holding it at your fingertips. Let everyone look at the candy and the string. While they are looking at it, place both your hands in your pockets, dropping the broken pieces in also. It's best to put both your hands in your pockets, because if you put one hand in your pocket, it will look like you're dropping something inside.

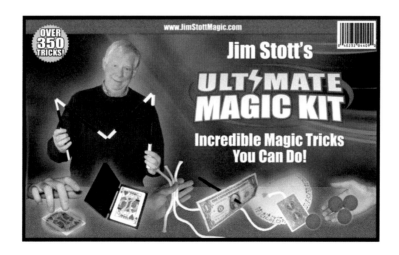

THE APPEARING KNOT ON THE ROPE TRICK

Hold a single piece of rope like this so your friends can see both ends.

Drop the end of the rope, while still holding onto the other end. Point to the end hanging down, take a bow, then look at the rope.

Oops... Nothing has happened.

Try it again, but still... nothing happens.

Then remember that your friends get to help by saying the magic word. When they do, you drop the end of the rope and there is a large knot tied on it. Thank your friends for being such good magicians.

HERE'S THE SECRET:

Before you start the trick, when nobody is looking, tie a bundle of knots near one end of the rope. Leave an inch or two sticking out.

This prepared rope can be kept in your pocket, backpack, lunch-box, book-bag, anywhere you can reach it easily and it stays out of sight.

To start the trick, hide the knot in your fingers so it doesn't show.

Your hand should look relaxed. If you're having trouble hiding the knot, make it smaller so it fits in your fingers better.

The first two times you do the trick, drop the end held between your fingertip and thumb. Keep the knot hidden. Pretend you made a mistake. This is a good chance to practice your acting skills.

On the third try, ask the audience to say the magic words. When they do, you appear to do the same move as before. But you actually do it in reverse. Hold the end firmly between your fingertip and thumb, then open your other fingers to let the knot end fall down.

Point to the knot, and pause. This pause is important, because it tells the audience that something has just happened, and it gives them time to notice the knot has appeared.

This trick can be done with something tied to the rope instead of a knot (as long as it will fit into your hand). For example, you could have a ring or small toy appear.

This is a fun trick that can be done almost anytime. Carry it with you everywhere, so you're always ready to amaze & entertain your friends!

RING ON & OFF THE ROPE

A solid bracelet is tied onto the string. Both ends are held by someone, then a handkerchief is draped over top of the bracelet. You reach under the cloth, and pull the bracelet off the string... MAGIC!

Step 1: The secret is the way you tie the string onto the bracelet. Fold the shoelace in half, then pull it through the bracelet (figure 1).

Step 2: Pull the ends through the loop at the middle of the string (figure 2), and pull it tight. This is how the ring is tied to the string.

Step 3: Have somebody pull the string, to make sure it is tight. Figure 3 shows what it looks like. Don't jerk on the string, or the bracelet may break.

Step 4: Have a friend or two hold both ends of the string loosely. Drape the handkerchief over the bracelet, making sure it can't be seen. Reach under the cloth, and pull the loop of string over top of the ring. (Practice with your eyes closed so you can do it perfectly.)

Pull the bracelet off the string, lift the scarf, and show it to your friends. Let them look at the bracelet, handkerchief, and string.

You can also do this trick in reverse: Have a friend hold both ends of the rope, then you cover the center with a scarf. Hold the bracelet under the scarf, and "tie" it onto the rope while the ends are being held. Lift the scarf to finish the trick.

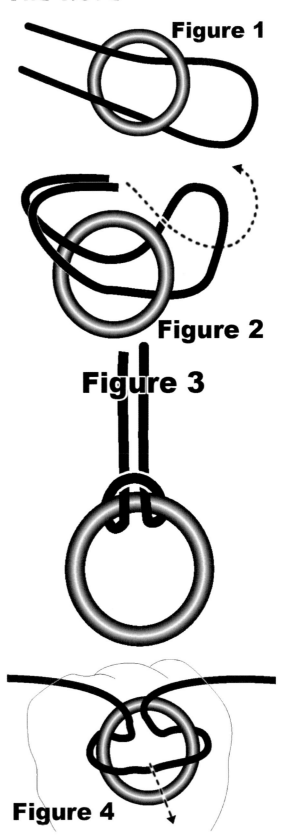

Figure 1

Figure 2

Figure 3

Figure 4

THE SHOELACE INSTA-KNOT

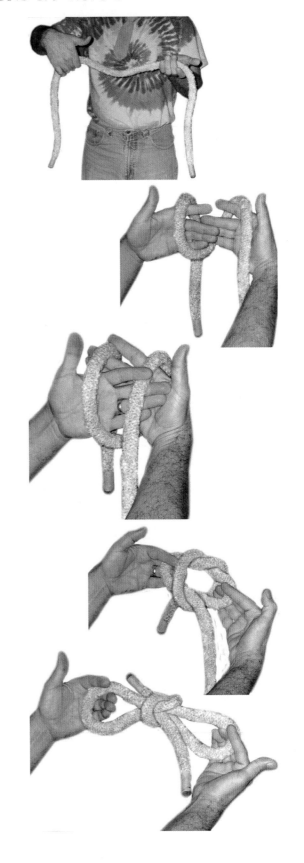

The magician holds a length of rope (or shoestring, ribbon, yarn) in his hands and pauses for a moment.

With a smooth movement, the hands are brought together, touch then separated. As the hands are moving apart, it's seen that a shoelace knot has appeared.

HERE IS THE SECRET:

You'll need a piece of rope. Shoelace, yarn, ribbon or thick flexible string will also work, but not thread or curly ribbons.

Start by holding the rope in your hands like you see in the top picture. Relax your arms. Make sure you're using the correct hand. The right hand holds it loosely like a hook, the left hand is palm up. Notice the amount of rope hanging down on the sides and in between the hands are about the same size.

Turn both wrists so the hands are now in position (2nd picture). These images are from the magician's point-of-view.

The first finger of each hand is raised up a bit so it looks like a lobster claw. The left hand is closer. The thumbs are not used.

Grab the rope with your first and second fingers, then squeeze tight. Keep your fingers as flat as you can, and don't use your thumbs.

Keep gripping the rope as you pull your hands apart. Don't try to do if fast, do it smoothly. Now you have a shoelace knot!

CUT & RESTORED ROPE

You've probably seen this trick before… the magician cuts a piece of rope in two, waves his hand over the parts, and they become one route again.

This is a classic of magic. There are hundreds of ways to do it. If you study magic long enough, you'll discover that every magician has a favorite method.

The envelope above has a notch cut on each end. This is for the rope to go through. These notches may be cut while the audience is watching. The holes on the front are cut before you start the trick, and should NEVER be seen by the audience. The holes are not cut all the way through the envelope, just one side.

Pull the rope through the envelope, but when threading the rope, slip it out and back through the hidden holes. Practice this so it's done smoothly, without the audience seeing it.

Lick the envelope and seal it. For a joke, pretend the glue tastes bad & make a funny face.

Now fold the envelope in half, and tighten the rope by pulling the ends. Not too much, don't tear the envelope.

Carefully cut along the fold. It will look like you also cut the rope. Put the ends of the envelope back together, wave the wand, say the magic words, wiggle your ears, then yank the rope out (tearing the envelope) and show it's restored!

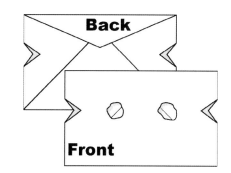

Back

Front

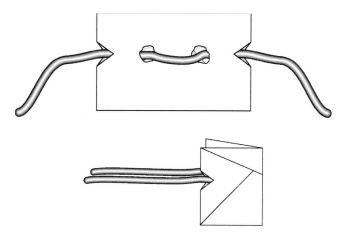

Cut here

Side View

WWW.JIMSTOTTMAGIC.COM

JUGGLING 1 · 2 · 3

ONE SCARF - Hold one scarf dangling from the center. Swing your arm across your body, and toss the scarf up and across.

With your other hand, reach up and catch it. Now toss it across your body to the first hand. Do this over & over & over. If you don't learn this step well, the others will be much harder.

Try to make each toss the same height. Study the drawings carefully.

TWO SCARVES - Hold one scarf in each hand. Toss one just like before, and when it gets to the top of the arch, toss the other scarf across your body. Catch the first one, then the second.

Don't toss both scarves at the same time. Wait until the first scarf is half-way to your other hand before tossing the second scarf. Remember the two scarf slogan: Toss-Toss-Catch-Catch.

THREE SCARVES - Hold two scarves in one hand (Black & White), one in the other (Grey).

Always start by tossing one of the two scarves. While that scarf is in the air, toss the grey scarf from the other hand.

Catch the white scarf, then toss the black scarf so your hand is empty to catch the grey scarf. Always catch with an empty hand. Don't place one scarf into another hand, always toss it across to your other side.

Jim Stott

MAGIC

www.JimStottMagic.com

THE RUBBER PENCIL

The rubber pencil is more of an optical illusion than a trick, but it still is fun to include in a magic show, especially if you are already using a pencil for some other trick.

First show the pencil is normal by tapping it on the table, or letting somebody look at it. If you can borrow a pencil, even better.

Hold the middle or the end of the pencil between your first finger and thumb tips. Now slowly twist your finger and thumb tips back and forth so the ends of the pencil go up and down. The ends don't need to move very far or fast.

At the same time you are twisting the pencil between your finger and thumb, slowly move your hand up and down about two inches each way. The pencil will look like is is bending, as though it were made of rubber. Watch yourself do this in front of a mirror, and you'll see how this looks very strange to an audience.

After showing the pencil looks like it is made from rubber, hand it to somebody so they can see it is actually a regular stiff pencil.

This could also be done with a pen, marker, small ruler, even your magic wand.

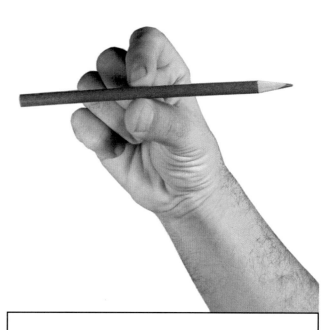

WWW.JIMSTOTTMAGIC.COM

HELPFUL HINTS...
PACKS SMALL, PLAYS BIG

There are many tricks and routines that can be done with small props carried around in your pocket.

That's one of the fun parts about learning magic... you're always ready to show your friends a quick routine that amazes and entertains.

When a magician says something "packs small and plays big", they mean it takes up very little room in their suitcase or pocket, yet it can be a really amazing and fun routine.

What does "play big" mean? There was a famous entertainer who did a great show with just a white glove on his left hand. That glove, with the addition of a couple of cardboard ears, became one of the most beloved rabbit puppets of all time. It's the performer that makes all the difference. In this case, Jay Marshall used his ventriloquist skills to bring "Lefty" to life.

A single piece of rope is a common item for magic routines. There are many wonderful routines that can be performed... cut & restored, knots appearing and disappearing, changing color, stretching, escapes. The magician Mac King does a great show with a piece of rope.

COLOR CHANGING PENCIL

After wrapping a pencil in a napkin, the audience says the magic words. When the pencil is unwrapped, it has changed color... or even better!

Spread the napkin flat on the table, corner pointing to you (pretend that it's home plate on a baseball diamond). Place the pencil in the middle so it's pointing towards 1st base & 3rd base. Point out that it's a yellow pencil (or whatever color yours is).

Unknown to the audience is an extra pencil hidden under the napkin. Same position, different color. Make sure nobody knows about it.

Wrinkle the napkin a little to hide the pencil underneath.

Grab both pencils and the napkin together, and start wrapping. It should look like you're wrapping just one pencil (the top one)

When you get to this point, with just the corners showing, turn the napkin over. Do this casually so it looks like you're still wrapping the napkin.

Wave your wand and ask the audience to say the magic words. While they're doing that, slowly pull the corners apart and show the pencil has changed color!

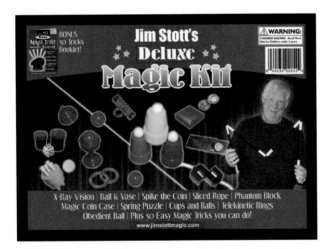

WWW.JIMSTOTTMAGIC.COM

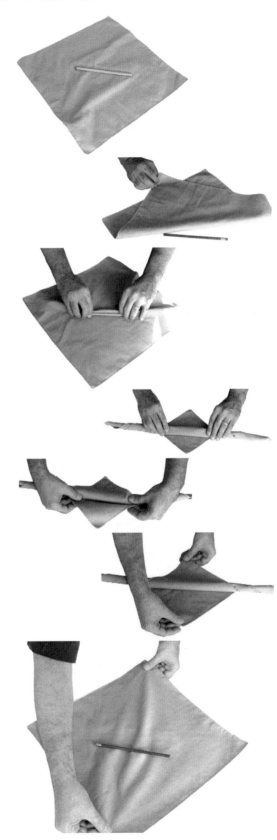

APPEARING PENCIL

The audience sees your empty hand holding a handkerchief (or a cloth napkin, paper towel, etc). Figure 1

Tell your audience to watch closely, something is about to happen. Don't tell them a pencil will appear though... that would spoil the surprise.

Gently clap your hands together, slowly lift the cloth (figure 2), and suddenly a pencil appears! Figure 3 This is a big surprise to the audience, and is actually easy to do. Of course, you still have to practice to make sure you can do it well each time.

Here's the secret: Before starting the trick, when nobody is looking, hold a pencil in your hand (figure 4). Palm up, pencil at the fingertips.

Notice how the eraser end is up, and sticking out above your fingers just a little bit. This is so you can grab it later.

Now drape the napkin over your hand, and position it so the corner is pointing towards your wrist, like figure 1. Make sure the pencil is held at your finger tips. This way it's hidden much better by the napkin. Keep your hand flat, and your thumb holding the cloth.

Turn your wrist to hold the pencil in a normal position (figure 3). Whisk away the cloth and reveal the magically produced pencil!

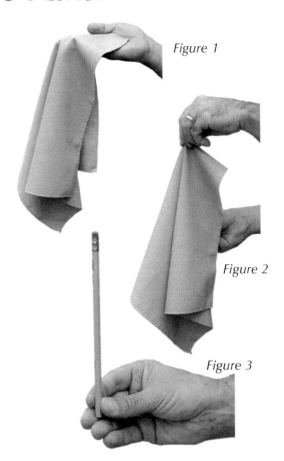

Figure 1

Figure 2

Figure 3

Figure 4

Grab the pencil thru the cloth, and lift both straight up. This is how it looks under the napkin

THE RISING PENCIL

Dropping a pencil into an empty plastic water bottle may seem a bit odd. Waving your hand over top and saying magic words might be even stranger. But when the pencil begins moving and floating by your command, you're magical!

HOW DOES IT WORK?

The pencil has a length of thread tied to one end. These photos show a thick string, but that's only so you can see it on the page. When you're performing this trick for an audience, use a thin thread. Also make sure it matches the color of your  shirt as closely as possible. Experiment with various colors and you'll discover which is the hardest to see.

Drop the pencil in the bottle, with the threaded end at the bottom.

The other end of the thread is tied to a button on your shirt, or your belt buckle. It needs to be long enough that you can hold the bottle, with the pencil inside, about a foot in front of you before the thread gets pulled tight.

By moving the bottle away from your body slowly, the pencil will be pulled up. Start by having the pencil move just a little, then a bit more, then rising slowly. Act surprised when it's floating.

This is a very fun trick to do, but it must be done carefully. Moving the bottle away from you should be performed smoothly and slowly. Use your body positions, hand, and eyes to keep people looking at the pencil.

Of course, this trick could be done with something other than a pencil. You could make a wand rise from the bottle, a skinny vase, or from your shirt pocket.

Combing two different types of illusion in this trick in turn it into a very interesting routine. At first, the pencil or wand is becoming animated. It moves around on it's own, as if it's alive. You could use the movements to illustrate a short story, or even us the pencil as a puppet who won't stop moving around.

Later in the routine, the pencil or wand levitates (floats)... a whole new trick in the minds of the audience!

As with all tricks, practice this one often and in front of a mirror.

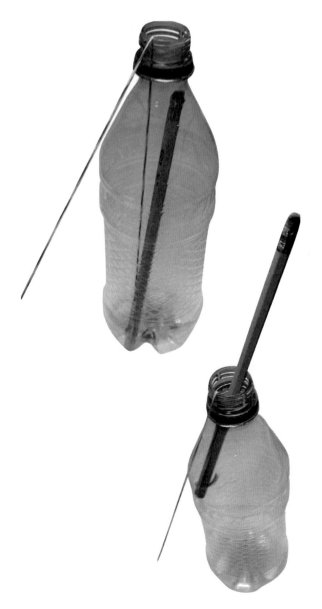

Jim Stott MAGIC

www.JimStottMagic.com

THE MAGNETIC FLOATING PENCIL

Holding a pencil in your fist, you explain that it has amazing properties. If you hold your arm really stiff, and don't move, the pencil will become magnetic and stick to your hand.

Grab your wrist with the other hand to steady your arm, and stare straight at the pencil held in your fist. Slowly open one finger at a time, until just your thumb is left holding the pencil. Pause for dramatic effect, then lift up your thumb to reveal the pencil sticking to your hand like a magnet!

The Secret: As you can see in the picture, your other hand is doing more than just keeping your arm steady. It's also holding the pencil.

Of course, make sure the audience does not see this part of your hand. Position yourself so the side of your body is towards them.

When you grab your wrist, your first finger straightens out and holds the pencil in place.

This should be done without anybody noticing. When you're practicing this trick, your goal is to grab your wrist and hold the pencil in one movement, so there are no suspicious adjustments or wiggling.

The rest is acting, and making it interesting to your audience. You can pretend like it is really hard to do, and you have to concentrate very hard.

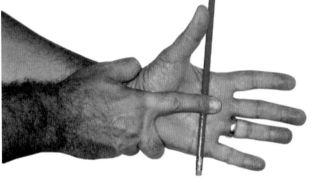

This same trick can be done with other things besides a pencil. If you have a magic wand, this is a great trick to include. You could also use a spoon, a stick, a straw, almost anything that will fit in your hand.

This is a fun and easy way to make a pencil float, and it can also be used for lots of other objects. However, it's not the only way. Making things float has been in the repertoire of magicians for hundreds of years. It's one of the most mystifying illusions of all.

But how? In the case of The Magnetic Floating Pencil Trick, your finger provides the lift. But wouldn't it be more amazing if you could let go of your wrist and still have the pencil stay in place!

If you have an extra pencil, wear a wristwatch and long sleeves, you can make it happen. Slip the extra pencil under your wristband (when nobody is looking, of course) and hide it under your sleeve. When you are holding your wrist, secretly slide the hidden pencil out until it's holding the pencil in your hand. Make sure the other end is still securely under your watchband. Now do the trick as before, with your hand holding your wrist while you slowly open the fingers to show the pencil floating. After a short pause, you can then let go of your wrist completely!

OPTICAL ILLUSIONARY TRICKS

The eyes cannot be fooled. It's the brain that is fooled. When something is seen by your eyes, it's your brain that figures out what it is. There are many ways to trick your brain.

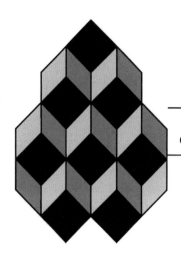

Do you see 6 or 7 boxes?

Looking at these dice can be very confusing!

Maybe there are alternate dimensions?

Is this a rabbit looking to the right, or a duck looking to the left?

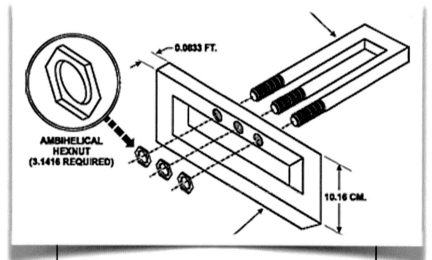

0.0833 FT.

AMBIHELICAL HEXNUT (3.1416 REQUIRED)

10.16 CM.

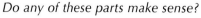

Do any of these parts make sense?

MAGIC IS A TRICKY BUSINESS

WWW.JIMSTOTTMAGIC.COM

COMEDY TRICK CARDS

If you've ever seen a magician with cards, you may know what this next flourish looks like. (A flourish is not a trick, but something that just looks flashy). A deck of cards is "sprung" from one hand to another, like a waterfall.

Most magicians use real sleight of hand, called "springing the cards". It takes time to learn, but it's not very difficult. Hold the deck in your hand, at the fingertips, and bend it inward toward your palm. Let the cards slide off the fingertips, holding them back at the thumb tips. Catch them by holding your other hand as though you were holding a baseball. Aim the cards towards your fingers. It takes practice... ideally over a table or bed to make it easier to pick up the cards that scatter. And they will.

The method on this page is easier, and you can use it to get a laugh in your routine.

As the picture shows, a few cards from the deck (about 40) are stapled together at the ends, so it zig-zags. Make sure you use an old deck and get permission.

Position your hands one on top of the other. Hold the trick deck in the top hand, and slowly let them drop into the bottom hand, one at a time. Even though you're not using sleight of hand, it still requires PRACTICE! As you get better, move your hands farther apart.

Here's how to get a good laugh using these cards. After the second time of dropping the cards from top to bottom, forget to catch them with the bottom hand. Let the cards hang free. Don't notice at first, pause, then see the cards and react. Pretend you've messed up the trick, and act embarrassed.

WWW.JIMSTOTTMAGIC.COM

COMEDY MAGIC MARKER

This is more of a joke than a trick, but to make it really funny, you need to act like it is an amazing magic trick.

Start by borrowing a marker from somebody, then tell the audience that you can turn this into a magic pencil. If nobody has a marker, just use one of your own.

Place the marker on the table, wave your magic wand, say the magic words, wiggle your toes, or whatever, then say that this marker is now a magic marker and will write in whatever color they name.

Have somebody name any color. Let's say it is red. Now pick up the marker, and get ready to write. Make it seem like you're getting ready for a great feat of magic.

When you have everyone's attention, quickly write the word RED on the paper in big letters, and hold it up for all to see. You may now hand out the marker and the paper for examination.

Here is another good trick that turns out to be joke. Tell a helper you have written a prediction of what they will say. Show the back of the paper, but make sure nobody can see through it.

Now ask if your helper knows what is written on this paper. When s/he says no, you turn the paper around and show the word NO in big letters.

Jim Stott
MAGIC
www.JimStottMagic.com

SILLY BALLOON-IN-BAG TRICK

Tricks with balloons are always fun for audiences, especially children. This balloon trick is a silly routine, perfect if your magician character does comedy magic.

On a table is a brown paper grocery bag. It's fine if the bag is a bit torn and wrinkled.

Open the bag, turn it upside down, and an inflated red balloon falls out. Watch as it falls, and bounce your head up and down as the balloon bounces. This will look very funny.

Place the bag on the table, open side up.

Untie the balloon, and let the air out. It will make a silly noise, so make sure you react to that. You could point to the balloon & say in a stern voice... " I heard that, say excuse me".

Hold the empty balloon up for everybody to see, and drop it into the bag.

Now comes another silly part of this trick.... lean over the bag, and blow into the top. Blow hard, as if you were actually blowing up a balloon. Keep your head above the bag. Stop now & then to catch your breath.

When you are done blowing, look into the bag, pause, then look at the audience and smile again.

Pause again, reach into the bag and pull out an inflated balloon. Hold it up for everybody to see, and take a bow!

Here is how this is done:

You actually have two red balloons in the bag at the beginning of this trick. Of course, they could be any color, just make sure that both balloons are the same color and size.

One balloon is kept in the bag with a little bit of tape. Or just hold the balloon in place with your hands when you turn the bag upside-down.

However you do it, make sure that only one balloon falls out of the bag when you turn it upside down. Also make sure the audience does not see inside the bag when you turn it. Keep the open part pointed towards you when you turn the bag over.

The balloon that falls out should be loosely tied so you can easily untie it and let the air out.

Another idea is to have an uninflated balloon fall out of the bag at the beginning. You blow it up, let the air out and then drop it into the bag.

The rest of this silly routine is just acting goofy and having fun!

On the outside of the bag you could write your magician name, or you could write "The World Famous Balloon Trick".

WWW.JIMSTOTTMAGIC.COM

GLOBAL HUMOR

If you can find a small globe, here is a funny gag to use sometime during a show. Small globes can be found at gift shops, and they are often used to save coins and sometime you'll find them with a pencil sharpener inside.

Ask a friend if he knows how to get to the nearest store. When they start to give you directions, tell them a map would make it easier, and pull the small globe from your pocket. Point to it, and say "We are here, and the store is there. But don't think you can get me lost, because I know that blue part is water."

Another gag you could use is this. When talking with someone, you might discover that you both know the same person, or you both have the same birthday, some sort of coincidence. When that happens, show the globe and say "It's a small world, isn't it!"

Here is popular one... When someone asks where you live, or you find out where they live, pull out the globe and say "That's easy to get to, it's only an inch and a half drive from here!"

Tell your friends you can read their palm, then pull a fake rubber hand from your pocket. Look closely and read a story from it, "Once upon a time there was a beautiful princess." (You won't have to read any more than that.)

Ask what is so funny, then turn the hand around so they can see the words, which proves you can read palms.

When you carefully and neatly write the words on the hand, use a marker, and be careful. Ink from the marker can be very messy.

Now tell them that palms are fun to read, but you liked the movie better.

Another joke is to ask your performing partner... "would you like your palm read?" When they say yes, paint their hand with washable red paint, or write the word "RED" in big red letters. Don't do this to a volunteer from the audience unless you've gotten their permission earlier.

Jim
Stott
MAGIC
www.JimStottMagic.com

You're So Funny!

Funny Comedy Gags

Here are some quick, funny gags, perfect for just about any show. These may also be useful as Scout meeting skits, talent shows, classroom assignments, etc.

Have a flower!

As the audience is entering, hand someone a flower (which is inserted into a straw).

By holding the top of the stem when they grab the straw, you walk away with the flower, and they are left with a straw.

This gag can also be used with a helium balloon on a short string tied close to your finger, and a long length of string held in your hand. The person taking the balloon ends up with the string.

With both these gags, it's a good idea to have a real flower, balloon or some other treat to offer so they don't feel cheated

Dusty, dusty, dusty!

This is a classic warm-up. Walk through the audience with a feather duster, apologizing for the dusty seats. Just as somebody is about to sit, gently dust off their seat, but get carried away, and start gently dusting off the person's head, hands, jacket, armpit.

The Highly Trained Flea

Performer in animal trainer costume offers to show her partner a trained flea for only five dollars, which is paid. He is asked to hold the flea's jacket, boots, and hat, which he does. Now the flea does many amazing tricks, such as jumping from one hand to the other, doing back flips, etc. There is actually no flea, only the animal trainer using her eyes and head "watching" how the flea is moving (pantomime).

When the flea is finished, the animal trainer applauds, then slowly realizes that she just squashed the flea. She starts acting very sad. The partner is not upset and says he never believed there was a flea in the first place. The animal trainer pauses, and asks "Then why are you holding the flea's clothing?" The partner gets angry, throws the flea's clothes down, and stomps off. The animal trainer smiles, takes a big wad of money from her pocket and counts it as she walks away.

Comedy First Aid

At some point a performer pretends to get hurt, and two other people come on with a stretcher to take him away. However, the stretcher is just two broom sticks with a blanket laid on top of them. Lay stretcher down, roll patient onto blanket, then pick up sticks and walk off. The gag is, the blanket and the patient stay on the ground while the two people walk off with just the sticks.

Use ambulance driver jackets, siren sound effects, flashing lights, and frantic movements. You might even find hats with battery powered sirens on top.

Funny Handshakes

This was made famous by the Marx Brothers. Whenever two clowns meet, they hold out their hands as though to shake hands, then lift their legs up into the others hand and shake each other's ankles. Many other variations could be developed... make your own!

www.JimStottMagic.com

WHERE DID THE SQUARE GO?

Here is a trick that's actually more of a puzzle. Be warned, however, that you're on your own to figure it out!

Trace or copy the large picture below, and cut along the dark lines so you have 5 separate shapes.

Re-arrange the shapes so it looks like this:

See the missing square in the lower right hand corner... Where did it go?

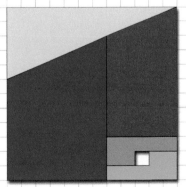

THE CRAYON TRICK

Who wouldn't love to see inside a closed box, especially around birthday time. This trick will make people wonder if you really can.

A spectator places any color of crayon into a box held behind your back. You can tell, without looking, what color is in the box.

Dump all the crayons to be used on the table. Now hold the empty box behind your back, and turn around. Instruct someone to place one crayon in the box. When they're done, turn around to face them, and pretend to concentrate, staring into their eyes.

What you're actually doing is scraping a bit of crayon off with your thumbnail. Bring your hand in front of you, and point to the audience. When you do, glance at your thumbnail to see what color the crayon is.

Try not to move your eyes though, because people will notice that. Instead, look at the audience, and move your thumbnail up towards your forehead. This will give you plenty of chance to see the crayon's color without everybody noticing your eye movement.

Announce in a loud clear voice what color he placed in the box, then place the closed box on the table and let everyone open it and look inside.

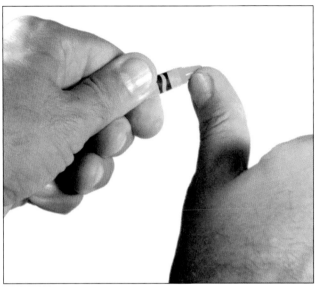

HELPFUL HINTS...

COSTUMES

The kind of clothing you wear when you perform is important. If you do a funny act, then you might want to get some old clothes that are too big for you. A hat is also a good thing to have. A jacket is handy, especially if it has a lot of big pockets that you can carry tricks inside.

Of course, you don't have to wear goofy looking clothes to do a comedy act. Some magicians do very funny shows wearing a nice suit and tie.

For a serious act, you'll want to look your best, with a nice suit, well combed hair, and a tie.

Costume clothes can be found at many secondhand stores. They are low priced, and there's plenty to choose from. Also keep an eye out for hats, ties, even suitcases when you are there.

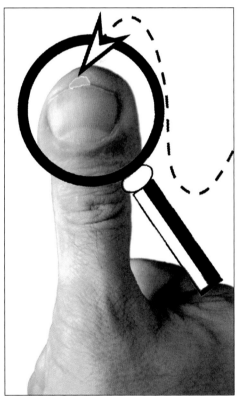

WWW.JIMSTOTTMAGIC.COM

CARDBOARD CARD PREDICTION

On the table is a piece of cardboard and a deck of cards. You explain to the audience that you will do this trick without touching the cards at any time.

Pick up the cardboard and have an audience helper pick up the deck of cards. Instruct them to place a card on the cardboard. You slide it off and begin making a pile of cards.

Have another card placed on the cardboard, then another and another. While the pile of cards is forming, tell them they can stop at any time, they can pull a card from the middle of the deck, they can even cut or shuffle the cards if they want.

When they decide to stop, you drop the cardboard on top of the pile of cards. Move your hands away, and ask somebody to please turn over the piece of cardboard. Written on the other side is a prediction. Now have somebody turn over the top card of the pile, and they match!

How does this work?

The reason your audience helper can cut, shuffle and use any card in the deck is because the predicted card is not in the deck at all.

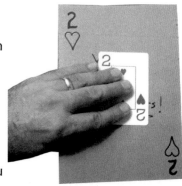

The whole time you're holding the cardboard and placing the cards on the pile, the 2 of hearts is held underneath the cardboard, hidden from view. When your helper is finished laying down the cards, you drop the cardboard on top of the pile. This places the predicted card on top. That's it! Just make sure the card is positioned the same way as the pile of cards.

There are a few details to keep in mind when doing this trick. When sliding the cards onto the pile, make sure you don't tilt the cardboard... people may get a glimpse of the card underneath. Practice this in front of a mirror so you can be sure the card is not showing.

Emphasize many times that you are not touching the cards, this will make the trick more powerful.

Wait until there are a few cards on the pile before you mention they can stop any time. If you tell them at the beginning of the trick, and they stop after one card... you have a problem.

If the pile gets messy to the point where there may be confusion as to which is the top card, ask your helper to straighten it out a bit. Remember, you don't want to touch the cards.

This is a great trick... practice & have fun with it!

WWW.JIMSTOTTMAGIC.COM

I Knew You'd Pick That

On the table are five cards and a folded piece of paper with a prediction written on it. The prediction is a secret, only you know what it is.

Thru a process of elimination, the cards are narrowed down to just one. When the prediction is opened up, it matches the chosen card. It seems that you can see into the future!

Here is the secret:

This is a useful technique for making the audience think they are choosing the card. In fact, it's the magician that makes the choice... which is why this technique is called "Magician's Choice".

Before the trick begins, you need to know which card you want the audience to pick. This is your "force card". Since they're face down, make sure you remember where it is on the table top.

Ask your audience helper to "point" to two cards. Don't say "pick" or they may pick up two cards which could spoil the trick.

Now you have two choices to make here, and this is where the secret of the trick comes in.

If your "force card" is one of the two pointed at, then place the other three cards into a pile on the side of the table. Leave your force card and the other one where they are.

If neither of the two cards pointed at is the "force card", then put those two cards onto the pile, leaving three untouched.

In other words, the helper does have a free choice of cards.... but you decide whether the cards stay or go.

There are now two or three cards left on the table. This time ask the helper to point to just one card.

Again, this card stays or goes depending on whether it's the force card. If it is the force card, move the remaining cards to the pile and leave the force card where it is.

If it's not the force card, move it to the pile and ask the helper to point to another card.

Eventually there will be one card left on the table. This is the force card. Turn it over so everybody can see.

Now have the helper unfold the prediction and show that they match!

Of course, this trick could be done with items other than cards. Three to five objects work best. Any more or less and you run the risk of the audience figuring it out.

PICK A NUMBER

Have a spectator choose any number between 1 and 63. Tell them to write it down and put the paper in their pocket.

Claim that you can tell what the number is by listening to the tone of their voice as they answer yes or no to the following questions.

Close your eyes (or put on a blindfold if you want to get extra fancy) and show them the first of these cards. Ask if their number is on the card. When they reply, pretend you are really concentrating. Show the next card, ask again. Do this for all 8 cards. When done, pause and then announce in a loud clear voice what number they picked... it's correct!

Here's the secret:

Notice the first number of each card, in the upper left corner. 1 • 2 • 4 • 8 • 16 • 32. These are special numbers, each double the one before it. Ask your math or computer science teacher, they can explain more about them.

All you have to do is add the special number for each card that the spectator replies "yes". For instance, let's say the chosen number is "45". The spectator will answer "yes" for cards 1, 4, 8 and 32. Add these numbers together and you get..... 45. As you are showing the cards, you'll need to know what the special number is on each one.

1	3	5	7	9	11	13	15
17	19	21	23	25	27	29	31
33	35	37	39	41	43	45	47
49	51	53	55	57	59	61	63

8	9	10	11	12	13	14	15
24	25	26	27	28	29	30	31
40	41	42	43	44	45	46	47
56	57	58	59	60	61	62	63

2	3	6	7	10	11	14	15
18	19	22	23	26	27	30	31
34	35	38	39	42	43	46	47
50	51	54	55	58	59	62	63

16	17	18	19	20	21	22	23
24	25	26	27	28	29	30	31
48	49	50	51	52	53	54	55
56	57	58	59	60	61	62	63

4	5	6	7	12	13	14	15
20	21	22	23	28	29	30	31
36	37	38	39	44	45	46	47
52	53	54	55	60	61	62	63

32	33	34	35	36	37	38	39
40	41	42	43	44	45	46	47
48	49	50	51	52	53	54	55
56	57	58	59	60	61	62	63

Copy this page on heavy paper, carefully cut out the cards. Ask an adult to help.

READING WITH YOUR FINGERS

What if you could read with your fingers? This trick shows that you can. Three people write their names on a piece of paper, a girl and two boys. The paper is then torn in three pieces, and the pieces are dropped into a box or hat. With a blindfold on, the magician is able to pull out the one girl's name.

Of course, this could be done with two girl names and one boy name, or two people wearing shoes with laces and one with velcro, or two people who take the bus to school and one who walks.

Here is how it works.

The paper is folded into three parts, and the names are written on the paper, like the picture. Now tear the paper at the folds, and drop the pieces in the hat. Cover your eyes with the handkerchief, and reach into the hat.

How do you tell which one is the girl's name? Feel the edges of the paper carefully. The name in the middle will be the only one with two torn edges. The top and bottom names have only one torn edge. Pretend you're thinking hard, and people will think you can read with your fingers.

MYSTICAL MOBIUS

With the use of a long strip of calculator paper, you demonstrate a very strange version of reality.

By taping the ends together (Figure 1), and cutting down the middle, you will end up with 2 loops of paper. That is expected.

Again, tape the two ends together of another strip of paper, cut down the middle... but now the loops are linked! (Figure 2)

The third time, you cut down the middle and end up with one large loop!

How does this happen?

As seen in figures 1,2 and 3, the number of twists in the loop makes all the difference.

The first loop has no twists when you tape the ends together. It helps the effect of the trick a lot to do this regular loop first. The audience can see and confirm that cutting down the middle results in 2 loops.

However, the second loop is twisted before taping the ends, but the audience must not be aware of it.

This is easy to accomplish, because the length of the paper strip hides any twists. When preparing for this trick, have the strips of paper laid on the table with the twists in place ahead of time. This makes it easier to proceed with the trick.

If you want to make the twists while taping the ends, you'll need to practice the move until it is done very smoothly. Telling a story of some sort will help keep attention away from the paper while you are making the twists.

The third strip of paper has two twists, as seen in figure 3. Again, cut down the middle.

It helps to have a line drawn end to end on the paper strips before starting. This can be done easily by laying the strip of paper on a table, putting a book at each end to hold it in place, then carefully drawing the line with a pencil and a yardstick.

Use safety scissors, and have an adult help. Or you could just tear the paper. Some papers will tear in a straight line, as well as certain cloths. You could make the loops from old newspapers, they are usually able to tear straight.

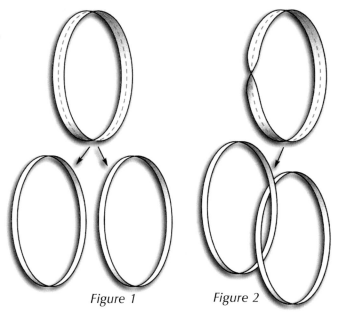

Figure 1   Figure 2

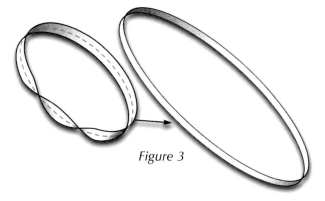

Figure 3

WWW.JIMSTOTTMAGIC.COM

THE GRAVITATIONAL COIN TRANSPOSITION TRICK

With two hands and four coins, you can make one coin travel thru the space between your fists and appear in the other hand.. is it teleportation?

This is what the audience sees: You show four coins and your two hands, like the photo above. Two of the coins go inside your fists.

The other two are placed on top of your knuckles by somebody from the audience.

After a bit of explanation about the effects of gravity on the coins, you pause and have the audience say the magic words. Upon opening your hands, one coin has traveled across!

Here is the secret:

During your "explanation" about gravity, you appear to drop the two coins from your knuckles to the table. Asking the audience helper to place them back on your fists, you continue on with the trick.

The helper has just done the trick for you!

When the audience sees two coins fall to to the table, they assume it is the coins that were on your knuckles. That's the secret to this trick.

When turning your fists over, the left fingers grab the coin on top of the left hand and hides it in the fist. This is pretty easy.

The right fist, however, does something totally different. It drops the coin from the top of the knuckles AND the coin from inside the fist. It must be done without visibly opening the hand.

By turning your fist sideways, you can hide the opening that allows the coin to fall out. This picture shows it from the magician's point of view:

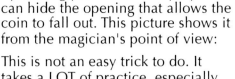

This is not an easy trick to do. It takes a LOT of practice, especially in front of a mirror. You must be able to do the moves without even thinking about them.

It must seem like the trick hasn't started yet when coins fall.

For instance, you could say.... "This trick that I'm about to do works by gravity. You know what gravity is, right? That's when things fall". Now drop the coins onto the table top. "Like that. Would you please put those back on my knuckles.... thanks."

Once those two coins are back on top of your knuckles, the audience thinks the trick is just starting. In fact, it's basically over.

Hold your fists wide apart, and move slowly. Any fast motion would look suspicious.

Keeping the fists apart, move them slowly up and down. With a slightly faster upward move, grab the coins into your fists, then bring them back down and hold still for a moment. This pause is very important.

Now slowly open your fists to show three in the left, and one in the right.

Again, this trick takes a lot of practice. But it's worth it. This is a great effect, and if done well, will fool everybody!

Of course, you're not limited to coins. You could also use game chips (like in the pictures), pebbles, small wrapped candy, any four objects that look alike and can fit in your hand.

MAGIC SHOW

www.JimStottMagic.com

MAILING A COIN BY MAGIC

Deciding to mail a valuable coin to your friend, you send it via magic express.

This is what the audience sees: You show everybody your valuable gold coin, and wrap it up in a piece of paper. After saying the magic words (with help from the audience), you tear the paper into small pieces and the coin is gone!

Here is the secret:

It's all in the way you fold the paper, plus a bit of sneaky misdirection at the end of the trick.

Start by placing the coin on the paper (figure 1).

Fold the bottom edge up (figure 2). The coin should not be visible. Make sure it's not peeking over the top.

Crease the folds as you're making them, and be as precise as possible. In this trick, neatness counts. (figures 3 & 4)

Both edges should be folded in the same direction, towards the audience.

This next fold is the one that makes this trick possible. You want it to look as though you were folding the top flap of an envelope (figure 5)

Notice how that fold creates a "pocket" where the coin is hiding. Don't let the audience see this. They should think that the coin is sealed inside. In fact, the pocket is open so the coin will fall out.

Which is exactly what you want it to do, but without the audience knowing.

By using misdirection, make them look at something else for a moment, just long enough for the coin to drop into your hand.

With that same hand, hide the coin while reaching for your magic wand. Drop the coin behind something or in your pocket, grab the wand and wave.

Pause, look at the paper, then slowly tear it into little pieces showing that the coin is gone!

WWW.JIMSTOTTMAGIC.COM

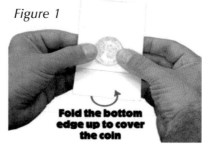

Figure 1

Fold the bottom edge up to cover the coin

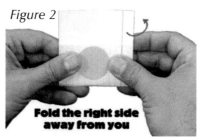

Figure 2

Fold the right side away from you

Figure 3

Fold the left side away from you

Figure 4

Fold the top flap down and away from you

Figure 5

Pocket with the coin inside

Let coin secretly fall into hand

Figure 6

PULLING A COIN THRU A NAPKIN

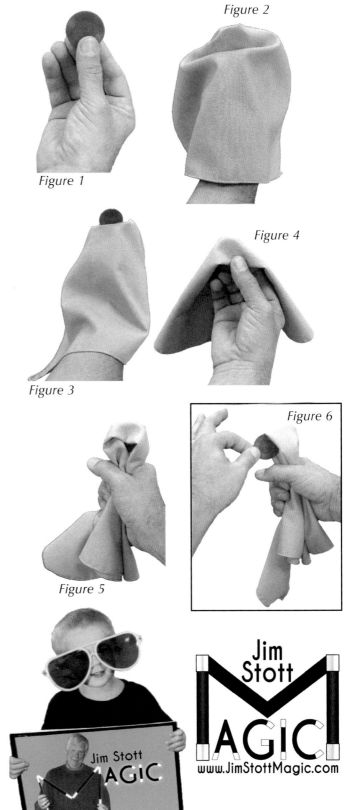

Figure 2

Figure 1

Figure 4

Figure 3

Figure 6

Figure 5

This is what the audience sees:

Show your audience a coin in your hand. You cover this coin with a cloth napkin or hanky, then show everybody that it's still there. Perhaps they think it's going to disappear. Twisting the bottom of the napkin, you ask somebody to hold it tight. As if by magic, you slowly pull the coin right thru the cloth... and show there is no hole in the napkin!

Here is the secret:

You don't actually pull the coin thru the napkin. By wrapping the coin in a special way, you make it look like it's in the middle of the cloth. The coin is actually outside the napkin, near the edge. Here's how.

Hold the coin (figure 1). This is important, so make sure you're hand matches the photo. Your hand will stay in this position for almost the whole trick.

Now cover the coin with the napkin, making sure the coin is in the middle. Again, this is important. If you want, you could have an audience helper place the cloth over it.

Now come the secret move.

While straightening out the napkin, you pinch some of it between your thumb and the coin. Figure 2 is from the magician's point of view. In other words... it's what you see, NOT what the audience sees.

Reach over the top of your hand, grab the bottom of the cloth closest to the audience, and lift it up to show that the coin is still there (figure 3).

Drape the napkin over your wrist, and straighten it out. Make sure there are no wrinkles.

Cover the coin again, but lift **both** layers off of your wrist, and place them over the coin. Figure 4.

Notice that the coin is now on the outside of the cloth, and is only hidden by the fold in the middle.

Straighten everything so it looks nice and neat.

Now hold the coin with one hand, and grab the bottom of the napkin (figure 5). Ask somebody to hold the napkin tight, making sure they don't see the coin peeking out from under the cloth.

You hold the coin in your fingertips, and slowly pull it out from under the cloth (figure 6). It will appear like it's being pulled right thru the napkin by magic!

Jim Stott Magic

Jim Stott Magic

www.JimStottMagic.com

VANISHING A COIN BAREHANDED

Sleight of hand magic - using pure skill to bring about a magical effect. With cards, coins, ropes and other small items, the magician can perform apparent magic.

It takes a lot of practice, and you're fingers may be doing things they've never done before. When you see a skilled sleight of hand artist perform, you may think it looks easy. It's not. But even though it's hard, it's worth it. Practice is the key.... lots of practice!

This is what the audience sees:

A coin (or any small object) is shown to the audience. Placing it into the other hand, and making a magical gesture, the hand is opened to reveal that the coin has vanished into thin air!

Here is the secret:

You don't actually put the coin into the other hand.

That may sound simple, but there is a lot more to it. The coin has to look like it went into the second hand. There has to be no doubt in the audience's minds.

Here's how...

Hold the coin like figure 1. This is a natural way to hold a coin, and looks quite ordinary.

Actually place it into the other hand, and close your fingers around it (Figures 2 & 3). Simple. Do this over and over until it seems like you're not thinking about it.

Now that you're tired of this, let's do it a bit different this time.

When you are turning your hand over to place the coin into your second hand, hold the coin with your thumb so it stays in your first hand. Keep your thumb on the coin for the rest of the trick, with your fingers flat.

Now pull your first hand back, still holding the coin, and close the fingers of the second hand at the same time. This should look just like it did when you were really putting it in your hand (figure 4).

Notice how the fingers are closed in figure 5. It looks like you're about to punch somebody in the nose (which is not nice). Make sure you close your fingers loosely like in figure 4.

To really make the audience believe the coin is in the second hand, look at that hand and move it up a little. Keep your focus on that hand. What about the first hand that is actually holding the coin? Let it drop down to your side, as though it was not even there. Don't think about it, NEVER look at it.

Say the magic words, pause, then open your second hand.... the coin has vanished!

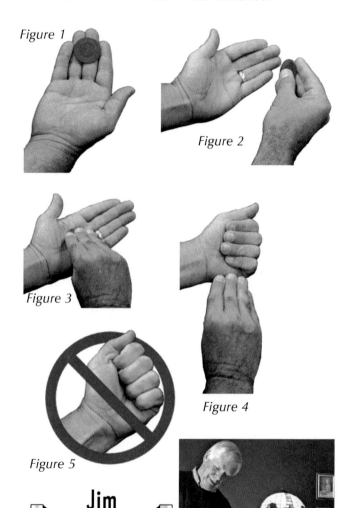

Figure 1

Figure 2

Figure 3

Figure 4

Figure 5

THE UPSIDE DOWN PRESIDENT

Borrow a dollar bill from somebody in the audience. Or maybe a twenty... who knows, you might get one!

Hold it up so the audience can see the picture of the president on the front, and point out that he is standing upright. Fold the bill a few times, keeping it held steady and in full view. When you unfold it, the president is now upside down!

Here's how it's done.

This one takes a lot of practice, because the sequence of folds is important.

These photos are from your point of view, what you will see when performing.

Pre-fold the bill, which makes it much easier to perform. Draw a dot on the back of the bill. This helps you know which part to grab at a crucial move.

Step 1:

While folding, keep the bill as motionless as possible. Act like it's "glued" to the air.

Step 2:

At this point, it helps if you hold the bill from the top, where the letter "N" is folded in half. Use just your fingertips so it doesn't look like you're hiding something. Fold the left side first, then the right. Having the bill already creased helps.

Step 3:

Before unfolding the bill, do the "magic move". It's always fun to get your audience involved by having them say the magic word, wiggle their fingers, maybe even do a silly dance. Use your imagination!

This part of the trick is the most important. Make sure you are unfolding the bill just like it shows in the photos.

Step 4:

The final move is where you reveal that the president's picture is now upside down.

If you finish and the president's picture is facing you, then try it again until you see the word "ONE" upside down.

Fold the top down (away from you) so it looks like this:

Step 1

Fold the ends (away from you) so it looks like this:

Step 2

Hold the corner with the dot and unfold (toward you) so it looks like this:

Hold this corner and unfold (toward you) so it looks like this:

Step 3

Reach over and grab the front of the bill (the part facing the audience) and pull up so it looks like this:

Step 4

ABRACADABRA!

WWW.JIMSTOTTMAGIC.COM

Rubberbands Are Jumping

While your audience is watching you stretch a rubber-band around your first two fingers, you talk about the famous Harry Houdini. No ropes could hold him, he always escaped.

Even when held tight (squeeze the rubber-band) he was able to jump right out. When you open your hand, the rubber-band has jumped to your other two fingers in the blink of an eye!

Here's how it works:

This is a very popular trick, and quite easy to do. Just pay attention to the photos and make sure your fingers are in the same position.

At the beginning you are stretching the rubber-band from one side of your hand to the other. This gets your audience used to seeing you stretch it, and it helps to focus their attention on your hands.

Before you close your fingers into a loose fist, stretch the rubber-band down along your palm to your wrist (figure 4). Make sure the audience does not see this part, so keep the back of your hand towards them. Also, keep the rubber-band against your skin, don't lift it up away from your palm.

Now curl all your fingers so they go inside the loop of the rubber-band. Keep you thumb out, and make sure all your fingers are inside (figure 5).

Notice that the fingers are straight, not bent over like a fist. This is important.

Slide the rubber-band up your fingers a bit so it rests on your knuckles. Again, hide this from the audience.

All these moves should be practiced so they can be done in one smooth motion.

Once the rubber-band is in position on your knuckles, you are ready to do the magic.

Make sure the back of your hand is facing the audience, and they can see the rubber-band easily (figure 2). Practicing in front of a mirror (which is always a good idea) will help a lot.

Pointing to the rubber-band helps to focus the audiences attention. You want them to know that something is about to happen, and they better be watching. As usual, pause before you do the next move.

To make the rubber-band jump across, open your fingers. It's just that easy! Make sure your fingers stay straight (figure 3). This happens very fast, which is why you want to make sure the audience is looking closely.

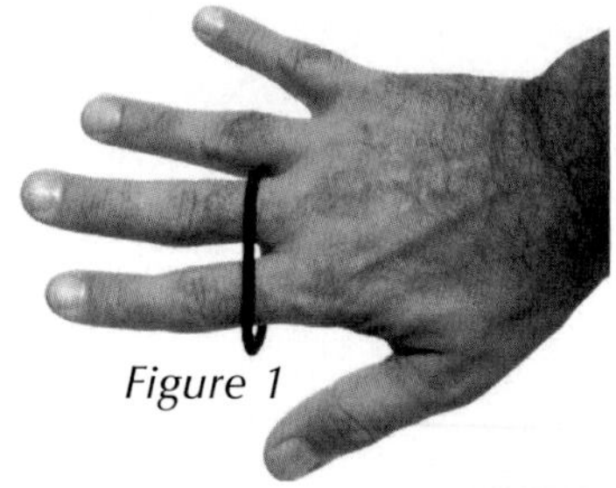

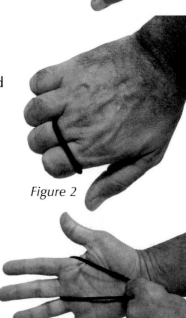

Figure 1

Figure 2

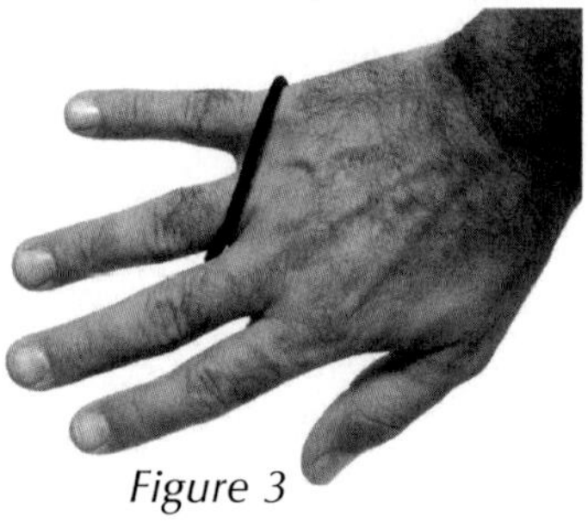

Figure 3

Figure 4

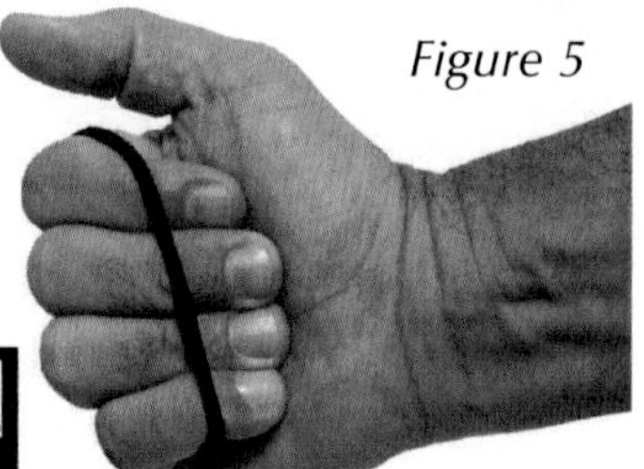

Figure 5

WWW.JIMSTOTTMAGIC.COM

FROM AN EMPTY BOX

After showing a box empty, you reach in and pull out... anything that will fit!

Many types of boxes will work, as long as they have a lid that is not attached. Look at the pictures on this page and you'll see why.

The item you want to produce, called the "load", is in a cloth bag tied with a string. That string is then attached to one side of the lid (figure 1).

The lid is placed on top of the box, with the load hidden inside (figure 2). Some of these pictures are an "x-ray" view so you may follow where the load bag is. The box you use should not be clear.

Begin with the box on your table. Slide the lid forward, towards the audience, keeping the load hidden (figure 3).

Turn the lid up & show the inside of it (figure 4). Rotate it if you want, showing the front & back of the lid. Make sure the string does not show. If the load is lightweight enough, a thin thread will work fine.

Drop the lid back down, then lift it up and back. As always, keep the load hidden (figures 5, 6, 7).

Once the lid is behind the box (figure 7), tilt the box   forward and show it's empty (figure 8). To put the lid back on, just do these moves backwards, open the box and pull out the items!

Practice with a mirror, and practice often! Keep in mind where the audience is, so you know what they can see. If they are too far to your side, they will see the load. Figure out a way to block their view.

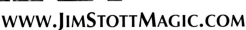

WWW.JIMSTOTTMAGIC.COM

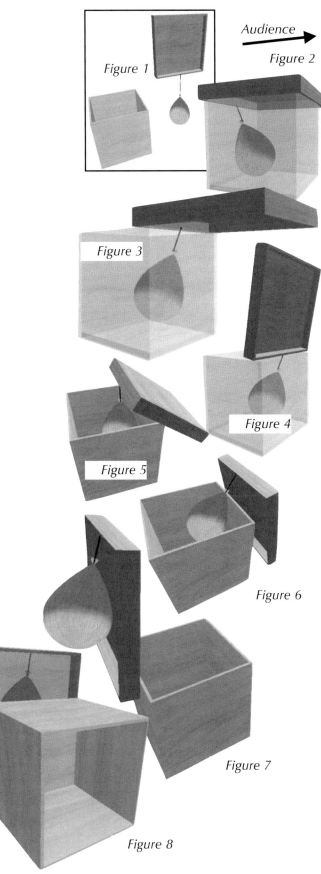

Audience

Figure 1

Figure 2

Figure 3

Figure 4

Figure 5

Figure 6

Figure 7

Figure 8

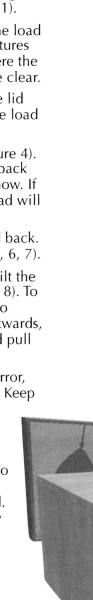

Two Panel Production

Two large sheets of cardboard are shown empty by the assistant, then placed together. When they are separated, a person appears between them!

Instead of cardboard, you could also use foam core. It's more expensive, but will last longer. You'll need to add supports to the panels so they can stand upright (unless you're using two assistants). The panels should be tall enough for a person to hide behind. Always slide them, don't lift them up to move. Downstage is towards the audience, upstage is away.

The Secret:

Follow the illustrations, and you'll see it's all in the sequence and position of the panels as they are being shown empty. The assistant moving the panels is on the right (stage left, wearing earrings in the illustrations), and the magician who will appear is hiding behind the panel on the left (stage right, wearing the hat). Of course this could be used to produce the assistant with the magician moving the panels.

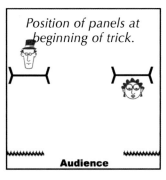

Position of panels at beginning of trick.

Audience

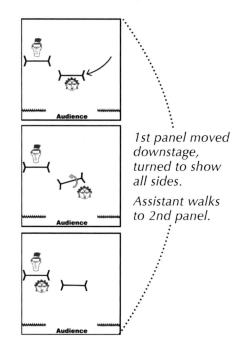

1st panel moved downstage, turned to show all sides.

Assistant walks to 2nd panel.

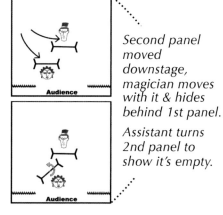

Second panel moved downstage, magician moves with it & hides behind 1st panel.

Assistant turns 2nd panel to show it's empty.

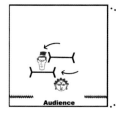

2nd panel slid towards the left (stage right), magician moves behind it and hides.

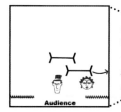

Panel slid towards the right (stage left), magician appears by magic!

www.JimStottMagic.com

MY POCKETS ARE FULL!

Once you begin collecting new tricks, and performing more often, you will need something to carry your show in. Since a beginning magician can hardly afford a $300 professional suitcase table, something cheaper will do. Actually, many professional use suitcases that were bought at secondhand stores.

Look around, and you will find many possibilities for cases that will match your show and personality.

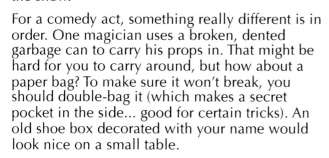

An old empty tackle box would work just fine. All those small compartments are perfect for holding cards, coins, rope, and any other items that you would use. How about an old lunch box. It's rugged, easy to find, not too expensive, and you can have a snack after the show.

For a comedy act, something really different is in order. One magician uses a broken, dented garbage can to carry his props in. That might be hard for you to carry around, but how about a paper bag? To make sure it won't break, you should double-bag it (which makes a secret pocket in the side... good for certain tricks). An old shoe box decorated with your name would look nice on a small table.

A perfect table for beginning magicians is a TV tray. They're lightweight, foldable, and sturdy enough to hold small tricks.

Jim
Stott
MAGIC
www.JimStottMagic.com

HELPFUL HINTS... SAVE YOUR IDEAS

Now that you've read and tried a few routines, you may already be coming up with ideas of your own. GREAT!! The best thing to do, when you have a new idea, is write it down in a notebook. Even if it seems silly and could never work, write it down. That idea may spark another idea that could become a great show.

Keep those notebooks. A magician in Atlanta started keeping notes in 1974. He now has enough material to write dozens of books and magazine articles, and develop lots of new shows.

Think about your idea, and try to picture it in your head. Now get the materials you need, and PRACTICE! You may know how to do the trick, but you still need to practice what you'll say, how you'll move, where you'll stand, everything that makes a routine entertaining.

When you're ready to perform for an audience, you'll feel confident and sure of yourself, because you will know exactly what is going to happen.

THERE'S ALWAYS MORE TO LEARN!

Magic is very popular and FUN. Everyone knows the name of David Copperfield, magician. He made the Statue of Liberty disappear, as well as a jet airplane. Criss Angel is well known for floating.

Some magicians tour with large stage shows. These are a real treat to see, and you may get to meet them backstage after the show.

Try to watch magicians whenever you can. Search the TV schedule, and mark the shows that have them.

There are many books about magic. Many can be found at your school or local library. Most magic books can be found around 793 in the shelves. Study them, and learn as much as you can about the fascinating world of magic. Also try juggling, puppetry, balloon animals, you could even be a clown.

STUDY HARD, KEEP PRACTICING, AND HAVE FUN!

Society of American Magicians:
www.MagicSAM.com

Society of Young Magicians:
www.MagicSYM.com

International Brotherhood of Magicians:
www.Magician.org

BOOKS

- *The Big Book Of Magic*
  by Bill Severn.
- *Now You See It, Now You Don't*
  by Bill Tarr.
- *The Amateur Magician's Handbook*
  by Henry Hay.

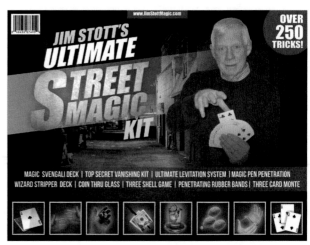

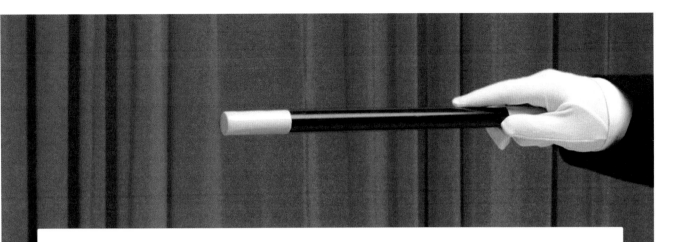

Thanks for reading *Learn Magic with Jim Stott!*

I hope you enjoyed the book and learned lots of fun and amazing tricks!

If you like the magic you have learned, I have created a secret web page where you can go to learn even more magic. To visit the secret web page, go to:

www.JimStottMagic.com/learnmagictricks.htm

If you would like to check out my magic kits, simply go to **Amazon.com**, Toys and Games, and search for 'Jim Stott Magic'.

Magic is a great hobby that you can enjoy regardless of your age! Have fun, enjoy, and thanks again!!

Made in the USA
Middletown, DE
20 June 2020